Woodturning
Forms and Materials

Woodturning
Forms and Materials

John Hunnex

GUILD OF MASTER CRAFTSMAN PUBLICATIONS

First published 2003 by
Guild of Master Craftsman Publications Ltd
Castle Place, 166 High Street,
Lewes, East Sussex BN7 1XU

ISBN 1 86108 355 6

Publisher: Paul Richardson
Art Director: Ian Smith
Managing Editor: Gerrie Purcell
Commissioning Editor: April McCroskie
Editor: Olivia Underhill
Designer: Fineline Studios

Production Manager: Stuart Poole
Colour origination by Universal Graphics Pte Ltd (Singapore)
Printed and bound by Stamford Press Pte Ltd (Singapore) under the supervision of
MRM Graphics, Winslow, Buckinghamshire, UK

Dedication

To the many woodturners throughout the world who
expressed their appreciation of my previous books.
Without their encouragement I would not have
contemplated undertaking this book. I thank you all.

Acknowledgements

To Mark Baker who offered me great support
for this endeavour.

To Olivia Underhill, my Editor, whose enthusiasm
for the project spurred me on.

To Stephen Haynes, Project Manager, who took
the trouble to look at my work in some detail to
understand what I am about.

Measurements

Although care has been taken to ensure that the metric measurements are true and accurate, they are only conversions from imperial; they have been rounded up or down to the nearest whole millimetre, or to the nearest convenient equivalent in cases where the imperial measurements themselves are only approximate. When following the projects, use either the metric or the imperial measurements; do not mix units.

Warning

Although woodturning is safer than many other activities involving machinery, all machine work is inherently dangerous unless suitable precautions are taken.

Do not use timber which may come apart on the lathe – beware of faults such as dead knots, splits, shakes, loose bark, etc.

Avoid loose clothing or hair which may catch in machinery. Protect your eyes and lungs against dust and flying debris by wearing goggles, dust mask or respirator as necessary, but invest in an efficient dust extractor as well.

Pay attention to electrical safety; in particular, do not use wet sanding or other techniques involving water unless your lathe is designed so that water cannot come into contact with the electrics.

Keep tools sharp; blunt tools are dangerous because they require more pressure and may behave unpredictably.

It is not safe to use a chainsaw without the protective clothing which is specially designed for this purpose, and attendance on a recognized training course is strongly recommended. Be aware that regulations governing chain saw use are revised from time to time.

Do not work when your concentration is impaired by drugs, alcohol or fatigue.

The safety advice in this book is intended for your guidance, but cannot cover every eventuality: the safe use of machinery and tools is the responsibility of the user. If you are unhappy with a particular technique or procedure, do not use it – there is always another way.

Contents

Foreword

I first met John some 14 years ago at a show when we had a chat about shapes and how the form is more important than having the best grain in the wood. I had heard of John and how he enjoyed working with shapes and form, but had not had the pleasure of meeting him until then. Such a conversation may not seem that memorable to many, but I was at the start of my turning journey and he also mentioned that he had picked up a piece and recognized it as mine by the pattern and finish on the foot area. This was a new concept to me – that people may have a style of turning.

John certainly has an individual style – he is always experimenting and never accepts conventional thought as sacrosanct. John has an inquisitive nature and is always looking at new ways of combining wood, shapes and textures to create a visual as well as tactile treat and is not averse to modifying tools to get them to work in the way that he needs them to.

John's passion and willingness to share is evident in his previous two books, *Woodturning: A Source Book of Shapes* and *Illustrated Woodturning Techniques*, where we can see his journey in woodturning and how he strives for beautiful shapes.

In this book John takes us a little further and shows us how, with a sensitive and thoughtful approach, we can integrate woods, texture and other materials to create something different without destroying the purity of form. I am sure that many turners will find this a helpful resource book. It will certainly be of help to those that are taking their first tentative steps into what is a fascinating and absorbing world. It may also challenge a few preconceptions from those further along in their journey.

Mark Baker
Editor, *Woodturning*
2003

Preface

The audience for this book would be turners who have mastered the basic
techniques and are perhaps looking for some ideas. There are many books and videos
giving advice on technique, but the information given is not 'gospel' – they are sharing
enthusiasm and experience. The advice offered may not suit your style of turning;
a tool that suits one turner may not suit another; a bevel that works for one person
may not work for another. We all work quietly in our own workshops on different lathes
with varying amounts of power; we all have favourite tools; we have different chucks,
and jigs that we have made for ourselves; we have our own way of doing things;
and we all develop our own strategies for turning.

My own philosophy is that technique should be your servant, not your master. Make it
work for you! It is the end result that counts, however you have achieved it. You can gain
great satisfaction from using your hands and eyes to make something.

John Hunnex
2003

Introduction

Images

Images seem to have a far greater impact on some people than words. Words seem to mean different things to different people; images are truly international with no language barrier to stop communication. Most people can instantly recall some image that has made a lasting impression on them. Images can intrigue, inspire and encourage us into action. They can also trigger off other ideas.

I own a classic woodturning reference book, *Das Drechsler Werk*, first published in Germany in 1940. I have never been able to read the German-language text, but I have always been able to enjoy and interpret the images.

Ideas

Imagination takes us into unknown areas. We have to try and work out our ideas and put them into form. When I was teaching photography at Goldsmiths College School of Art in London, many of my colleagues prized imagination and ideas above technical skill. Technique can be taught, technical skill can be acquired by constant repetition, but ideas exist only in our own minds.

Ideas pop in and out of our heads all the time. They are very elusive things. Where do they come from? Ideas about how to overcome a problem are often born of necessity. You ask yourself 'How can I overcome this difficulty?' You work things out as best you can with the materials to hand. Our imagination runs free, but we have to try to put form to this idea. The most ingenious idea will fade unless you are able to put it into practice.

Ideas are generally influenced by personal experience. Some of the best shapes for vessels were produced in stone and clay thousands of years ago and probably arrived out of necessity. There are some outstanding examples of these in The British Museum and I have been fortunate enough to have had the experience of seeing them, which has strongly influenced my woodturning.

When you do get an idea, try and capture it on paper before it floats away. The roughest outline will do – you don't have to be an accomplished draughtsman. Once you have got it into some form of concrete image, you will be surprised at how many ideas will spin off from it. You will go off in all sorts of directions!

Where appropriate I have tried to explain how I have achieved some of the effects shown in the illustrations. However, from my experience over the years of talking to turners, both from the United Kingdom and other countries, I know that they have their own ideas on how to solve problems and achieve different effects.

The idea behind this book is to take ten basic themes, and to explore the possibilities within each theme.

Using different woods together

Wood can be very decorative in its own right but can also be quite bland. It can, however, be combined with other woods to make interesting contrasts.

When I combine woods, I always try to imagine the work in a few months time, when the tone of the wood has changed. Some woods, like yew, mulberry, or padauk, for example, can be quite spectacular when first turned, but after a few months' exposure to ultraviolet light, the patina changes and they tone down quite considerably. If I am producing work for an exhibition I keep it for quite a while before showing it so that I am not misleading the audience.

One thing you have to watch when combining woods, is to match the grain structure. If you use cross grain with long grain it can cause problems, as the wood may move in two directions as it is drying.

Care must be taken when gluing surfaces together. The surfaces must be as flat as possible and the adhesives carefully applied as some of them can produce stains and ugly lines. Careful clamping and weights can help.

SPALTED BEECH, PADAUK AND BLACKWOOD BOTTLE

H: 8½in (216mm)   D: 5in (127mm)

This hollow form is one of my favourite shapes. I find cutting the curves leading down to the base and up to the top some of the most challenging and satisfying turning for me.

I wanted also to combine strong contrasts of colour within the shape.

It was turned in three, the spalted beech base being the first. Collar joints were used between sections; these joints make for safer and stronger joining. The padauk section was then glued on and turned. Finally the blackwood top was turned separately and added before sanding and finishing the whole piece.

SPALTED BEECH WITH BLACKWOOD RIM
CLOSED FORM

H: 4½in (114mm)   D: 12in (305mm)

This striking piece of beech was heavily spalted and
I wanted to pick up the black lines of the spaltering and
complement them in the rim. Blackwood seemed the
most appropriate wood to do this.

I use collar joints when combining woods as this gives
strength. I kept the rim quite delicate, as the wood in
itself was dramatic and I did not want it to overpower
the piece.

PLYWOOD AND MAHOGANY HOLLOW FORM

H: 5in (127mm)   D: 13in (330mm)

Using a layer of mahogany between the structured plywood allowed me to give an impression of a crisp edge to this hollow form.

Plywood can be rather difficult to turn because, although the outer layers are of good quality veneer, the inside layers tend to be of a poorer quality and can have defects which may show up in the turning.

I also added a mahogany top for the same reason, and to give more emphasis to the hollow form.

A BOWL WITHIN A BOWL
ASH AND ELM

H: 7½in (191mm)   D: 7in (178mm)

This is made from two pieces of wood. The smaller bowl contained within the larger bowl is figured ash and the outer bowl is burr elm.

The idea was to have a strong contrast between the interior and the exterior – one bowl nesting and glued inside the other. I turned the outer bowl first to give me the dimensions I needed to turn the inner bowl, and left the rim of the inner bowl standing proud above the softened rim of the outer bowl.

FLAME-FIGURED ELM AND BOXWOOD BOTTLE

H: 8in (203mm)   D: 5½in (140mm)

I turned and hollowed the bottle shape (using a hook tool) from a lovely piece of flame-figured elm. I parted off the top and inserted a rim of boxwood. The piece I had parted off was then replaced and finished with another rim of boxwood.

As boxwood is generally only available in small sizes it's good to be able to use it in this way, the beauty being that it picks up some of the warm yellow tones in the elm.

SAPELE, MAHOGANY, SYCAMORE AND PURPLEHEART PLATTER

H: 1½in (38mm)   D: 14in (356mm)

This was a very simple platter, almost flat across the plane.

While the wood was still in 'square' form I drew the dimensions and cut where I wished to insert the first strips of contrasting wood. These were glued together and left to dry. When dry, I then cut the second line and inserted the strips of contrasting wood. When the whole square was dry, I cut a circle of about 14½in (368mm) in diameter on the bandsaw and turned in the usual way.

It was a time consuming process: each section had to be thoroughly dry before proceeding to the next stage. I used only seasoned wood for this platter.

CHERRY, PURPLEHEART AND BIRCH PLYWOOD STRIP BOWL

H: 4in (102m)   D: 6½in (165mm)

I wanted to add a little interest to a seasoned cherry blank that had been keeping for a few years. I knew the shape I wanted to turn, and so I cut the blank into two thirds/one third. I then glued and inserted first a strip of very thin birch plywood, then a thicker strip of purpleheart, and the final strip of thin birch plywood. The blank was then all glued together and clamped and weighted for quite a few days before I turned the piece.

I think the strip emphasizes the shape of the bowl as well as adding decoration to a piece of plain wood.

BROWN BURR OAK AND BOXWOOD FLASK

H: 10in (254mm)   D: 3½in (89mm)

As the brown burr oak is long grain, I screwed a faceplate directly into the base. I use longer screws in long grain than I normally use in cross grain; this allows me to use more pressure when hollowing the piece.

I used a short bed lathe as it enabled me to work in front of the piece without the restriction of bars. I also had a foot control to stop/start the lathe as it is safer when working on long, hollow forms. It is very difficult to remove a deep hollowing tool from a piece of work while it is spinning at speed!

I used a piece of boxwood which allowed me to come right down to the narrow opening I had designed to complete the shape of this piece.

ASH AND BRAZILIAN MAHOGANY WIDE-RIMMED BOWL

H: 3in (76mm)   D: 14½in (368mm)

The deepest part of the bowl is Brazilian mahogany and I laminated a wide rim of rippled ash onto the bowl. Any kind of lamination always requires patience, a good adhesive and plenty of clamps and weights!

The rippled ash had a very strong grain pattern and, with the contrast of light and dark colours, made this an interesting piece to turn.

FIGURED BEECH AND IROKO BOTTLE

H: 11in (279mm)   D: 7in (178mm)

The beech had a strange figure to it, producing warm brown shades, signifying that it was beginning to rot.

I wanted to combine the base with another wood at the top, but did not want it to compete too strongly with the colour of the beech.

I found a piece of iroko which seemed to continue sympathetically with the tone of the base. The top was inserted and glued using my usual collar joint.

PITCH PINE AND COCOBOLO BOTTLE

H: 7in (178mm)   D: 7in (178mm)

This is a combination of an inexpensive wood – pitch pine – and an expensive wood – cocobolo. Both woods mellow to nice warm tones.

The bottle was hollowed out from the pitch pine, which made the reddish/brownish streaks form a strong pattern. I wanted to pick up the same tones in the spout of the bottle and chose cocobolo to complement them.

COCOBOLO AND EBONY RIM
CLOSED FORM

H: 4in (102mm)   D: 9in (229mm)

Two of the most beautiful woods are brought together
in this piece. Rich, dark colours and lovely texture
combine to make this one of the most satisfying forms
I have turned.

I used a simple collar joint to glue the rim of ebony
to the closed form made of cocobolo. The black rim
gives strong definition to the edge of the piece.

Surface texture

Textured surfaces can be achieved by using special tools, or sandblasting away soft fibres leaving more interesting harder fibres. The difference between using sandblasting and the tools for texturing, is that sandblasting discriminates and only removes soft fibres; the texturing tools are indiscriminate and will texture all the surface of the wood.

I use the services of a professional sandblaster who works in a pressurised cabin with powerful compressors. He has the necessary equipment to quickly remove the soft fibres from wood, leaving the older growth in relief.

Scorching wood has a similar effect as sandblasting, in that only the soft fibres are removed. The wood does get charred in the process but this can be buffed to give a wonderful gleam to the surface.

Sprayed work often covers very bland wood and just emphasizes form. Sometimes wood becomes stained during growth and this can distract the eye from the form. This would be a suitable case for spray painting.

Texturing surfaces may seem to depart from the tradition of the smooth polished surfaces that we associate with wood, however, tradition should be our stepping stone, not our millstone.

WHITE ASH HOLLOW FORM

H: 6in (152mm)   D: 10½in (267mm)

I rough-turn most of my work to about 1in (25mm) and leave it to dry for approximately a year. During this time, it will generally distort and ovalize quite noticeably.

After a year I remount the work on the lathe for completion; leaving it at about 1in (25mm) enables me to reduce the distortion to a round shape.

Ash sandblasts very well, as it has quite a dramatic pattern to the grain structure; I find white ash benefits particularly from this treatment.

ASH DISCUS VASE ON STAND

H: 21in (533mm)   W: 16in (406mm)

If you select your wood carefully, looking at the grain structure, you can achieve some very interesting effects using sandblasting. There was a lot of movement in the grain of this ash so, to get the best out of it, I turned some discus shapes and mounted them on a stand.

ASH TEXTURED BOWL

H: 2in (51mm)   D: 8½in (216mm)

The textured surface was created using an Arbortech Mini Grinder which is attached via an extension arm onto a 4½in (115mm) grinder.

The ash bowl was cut and sanded before carving, and the grinder was drawn carefully across the rim of the bowl at about 60 degrees while the lathe was running.

In order to achieve a strong contrast between the smoothness of the bowl and the texture of the rim, liquid leaf gold metallic paint gave a fine effect. The final finish was two coats of Danish oil on the rim and underside of the work.

SANDBLASTED ELM HOLLOW FORM

H: 7in (178mm)   D: 9in (229mm)

Elm is a tough wood to sandblast, so the work must be completely finished before I take it to the sandblaster as there is no returning it to the lathe afterwards.

Sandblasting does have the effect of drying out the wood and reducing it to one tone, so I oil the work at the end of all the processes to give it a surface finish that can be kept clean, and to restore some warmth to the tone.

ELM VASE ON COCOBOLO BASE

H: 10in (254mm)   D: 4½in (114mm)

I wanted a contrast between rough and smooth, and light and dark in this piece. I turned and hollowed the elm vase, texturing the centre but leaving the top and bottom smooth. I left a 'spud' on the base so it could be mounted into a base of darker cocobolo wood.

LARGE GREY STONE-FLECK VASE

H: 11in (279mm)   D: 8in (203mm)

The wood used for this piece of work is structured birch plywood.

The surface is a grey stone-fleck spray paint, with a very durable tough finish when it is dry. Used mainly in interior decoration, it is a plastic-based paint, and is available from hardware stores and woodturning catalogues in a variety of colours. The stone flecks give a rough stipple finish which is strongly textured.

When using sprays, I find it easier to keep the piece 'on the move', so by using a piece of old wood fixed to a revolving 'lazy susan' mechanism, I can continually turn the piece while spraying.

SPRAYED PLYWOOD FLASK

H: 10in (254mm)   D: 13in (330mm)

This was structured from plywood, as described later
in 'Using different plywoods' (see pages 87 to 99).
Once finished, it was sprayed with paint that
incorporated flecks of stone to give a textured surface.
The paint colour was rather insipid and so I finally
finished it with a maroon metallic car paint spray.

LARGE TEXTURED ELM LIDDED CONTAINER

H: 12in (305mm)   D: 10in (254mm)

I turned and hollowed the base of this lidded container and kept a piece from the same block of elm to turn this hat-shaped lid.

The texturing was made using a fine gouge with a cutting and lifting action while it was on the lathe. The attractive grain pattern is still visible through the textured surface.

NATURAL TOP SCORCHED ASH VASE

H: 7½in (191mm)   D: 6in (152mm)

This was hollowed in one piece (using a hook tool), leaving the natural bark of the ash branch to form the top of the vase.

The scorched effect was achieved with a gas blowtorch which removed the soft fibres. The remainder of the wood was charred but once it had been finished with Danish oil it was buffed up to give a soft gleam.

RIBBED-TOP OAK BOWL

H: 2in (51mm)   D: 6in (152mm)

The interesting grain pattern of this oak is emphasized by using a gouge to cut coves on the top rim.

The ribbing has given strong movement to the granular structure of the wood.

BURR MAPLE TEXTURED BOWL

H: 5in (127mm)   D: 5½in (140mm)

I deliberately left the bark inclusion in this piece of maple. It gave impact, and added to the rugged character rather than the sleek polished items we usually associate with maple.

The texture across the rim was achieved by carefully and slowly drawing a chain saw across the top of the work. The texture on the main bowl was produced by using a fine gouge.

BEECH VASE

H: 5½in (140mm)   D: 5in (127mm)

This beech vase was textured using a tool specially designed by a tool manufacturer. It gave me full control of the degree of texturing I wanted. In this case I wanted a slightly more delicate texture than that created by the Arbortech Mini Carver on the angle grinder. You can repeat the process until you get exactly the degree of texture you want.

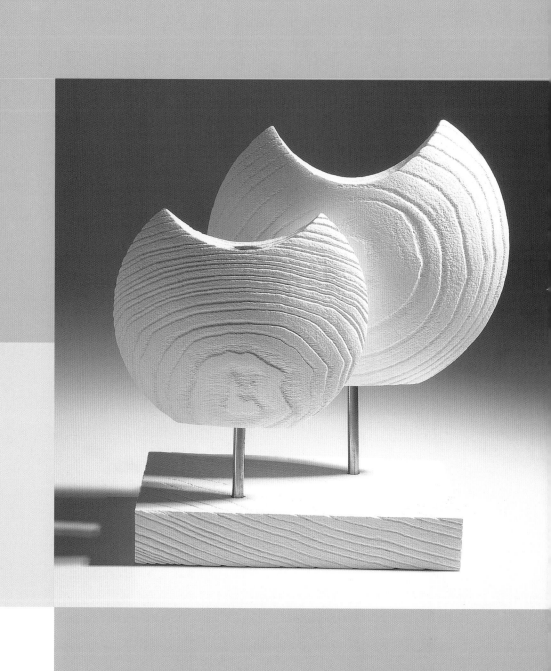

Combining work in pairs and groups

We normally associate faceplate turnings with solo items and most of the illustrations in this book confirm this view. I thought I would move in another direction and produce work that is linked in some way, i.e. pairs, trios and group work.

Functional items have been paired off, such as candlesticks, condiment sets, and so on, but decorative items usually stand alone.

The pieces have to be designed as a 'whole' to begin with, otherwise they just look as if they have been placed together as an afterthought.

This idea can lend itself to all kinds of turnings provided you keep in mind the fact that each piece you turn is part of the 'whole'.

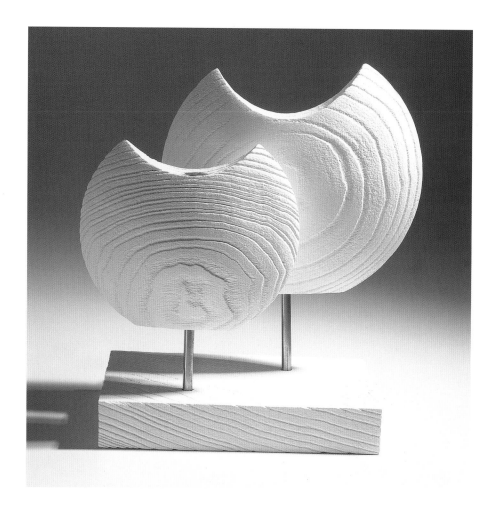

SANDBLASTED ASH DISCUS VASES

H: 10in (254mm)   W: 12in (305mm)

The discus shapes are turned both sides using a spigot. The first spigot is removed when the work is mounted on the second spigot. The second spigot is removed by using wood jaws to hold the piece on the lathe.

The top shape is turned by cutting the ash disc to create a flat base, which is mounted on a very small faceplate. This allows the top shape to be curved by cutting inward rather than just cutting a shape on a bandsaw.

When the discs are finished, a hole is drilled down the centre, wide enough to take a glass tube to hold flowers once completed. They are then ready for sandblasting, before finishing with white acrylic paint and mounting on a base with stainless steel rods.

SANDBLASTED ASH DISCUS VASES

H: 12in (305mm)   W: 14in (356mm)

The extreme contrast of black and white is always eye-catching. The centre disc was to provide the contrast and so this was stained black.

When you are working on a theme, other ideas come into play and it is good to extend the idea until you feel you have exploited it to its full capacity. It is then time to move on to find fresh inspiration!

WALL PLAQUE

H: 14in (356mm)   W: 26in (660mm)

When I exhibit woodturning, I am invariably required to use the wall space as well as the floor space in a gallery. People are quite intrigued to see wood on the wall instead of paintings, drawings, or photographs! This is a wall plaque made up of a variety of woods, both native and exotic. The discs were individually turned and finished.

Once I had decided on the arrangement I liked, each disc was dowelled and fitted into position. This idea can be extended in a number of ways with different arrangements of patterns and backgrounds.

FIGURED BEECH DOUBLE DISH

H: 6in (152mm)   D: 13in (330mm)

The two off-centre dishes were cut from the same piece of figured beech. The work had to be carefully measured, so that the smaller dish nested into the hollow of the larger dish.

I continued the linking theme by lining up the grain pattern on the two dishes.

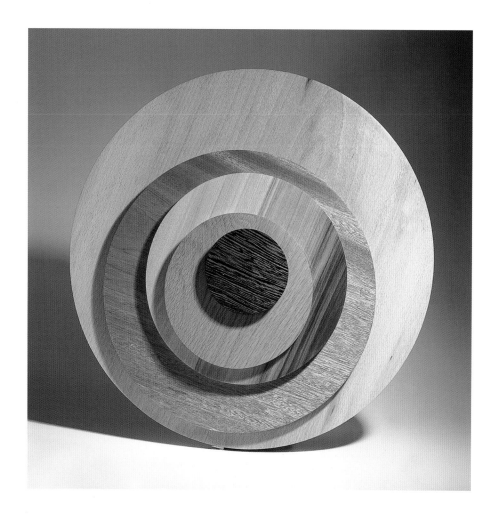

DISC CIRCLES WALL PLAQUE
VARIETY OF WOODS

H: 18in (457mm)   D: 18in (457mm)

The off-centre arrangement and the combination
of light and dark woods presented quite a challenge.
Each disc was off-centred to the previous disc. The
strong colour difference on the third disc (parana pine)
added to the interest. The juxtaposition of grain running
crosswise and lengthwise kept the feeling of continuous
'movement' within the piece.

ASH TRI-POT

H: 12in (305mm)   W: 6in (152mm)

As a photographer, a tripod is an essential part of my daily life, which gave me the idea of producing tri-pots. This work brings together two of my abiding interests — woodturning and photography.

The pots are connected by dowels drilled into the base; the bases were left a little thicker than the body to allow for this drilling.

OAK TRI-POT

H: 9½in (241mm)   W: 7in (178mm)

The goblet-shaped tops were given a small rim and tapered down to a fine stem. The linking steel had to be placed at the thickest part of the stem to avoid cracking.

This was a nice-coloured oak which was given several coats of Danish oil to give it a warmer tone finish.

WATER TOWERS

H: 12in (305mm)   W: 17in (432mm)

Once you start thinking about groups, you begin to
look for them. I saw a water tower on a hill and thought
it was a very interesting shape.

I was inspired to turn a group of them in structured
plywood. They are hollow and connected by stainless
steel rods.

LOLLIPOP LANDSCAPE
VARIETY OF WOODS

H: 12in (305mm)   W: 16in (406mm)

Why shouldn't we indulge in a bit of fantasy now and again! We often see groups of trees on a hillside and this was the impression I was after when I produced this piece of work. Rather than make it representative of trees, I tried to give the impression of trees.

It was a great way to try out different species of timber and I must acknowledge the help that Craft Supplies in Derbyshire gave me with this project. There are 28 different species of wood in this work – turned, finished and mounted on dowel rods inserted into a piece of burr elm.

This piece proved very popular with children!

CLOUD LANDSCAPE
VARIETY OF WOODS

H: 12in (305mm)   W: 12in (305mm)

I followed on from the Lollipop Landscape with
Lollipop Clouds. The discs were larger: approximately
3½in (89mm) in diameter. Cloud formations are always
fascinating and sometimes appear to be in layers.

Again, it was a good exercise to try out the wide variety
of woods that are available to us.

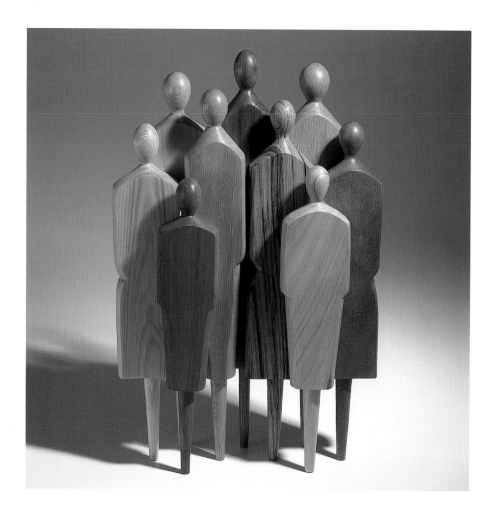

PEOPLE
VARIETY OF WOODS

H: 14in (356mm)   W: 12in (305mm)

Figures have been turned in wood many times before but most of them appeared to be toy-like. I wanted to keep the figures simple while retaining a little dignity.

The most obvious groupings to us are people. We all have to establish links to some group or the other, whether we like it or not!

These spindles are made by turning them directly between centres on the lathe – they were not cut on a bandsaw first. The spindles were turned to give an impression of people rather than a representation. I have kept the shape as minimal as possible.

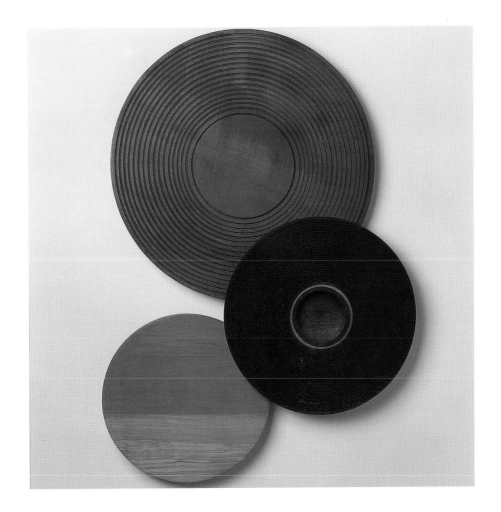

SYCAMORE, BEECH AND ASH
PLANET PLAQUE

H: 26in (660mm)   W: 17½in (445mm)

This was inspired by computer graphics shown on a television programme relating to space. I admired the strong colours and the rings drawn around the images.

I also particularly liked the overlay of colours giving the impression of floating clouds, and I used different dyes to achieve this effect.

The largest disc is sycamore, the middle disc is beech ebonized and dyed purple in the centre. The smaller disc is ash, first dyed yellow and then overlaid with grey dye.

Incorporating other materials

We can sometimes incorporate other materials into our work: rope, leather, metals, resins, dyes, and so on, have all been used to good effect.

When using rope, I try always to use natural sisal. It seems more comfortable with wood than synthetic ropes. If you wish to colour the rope, sisal responds well to spirit-based dyes. Water-based dyes have a tendency to make rope 'swell'.

Sometimes you have to rely on the skill of others to help you. The metal stands I use are produced by other craftspeople and are readily available in craft shops.

Looking around our everyday world can sometimes give you an idea. I saw heavy studs in an old oak door and thought how effective they looked and included them in a piece of work (see page 46).

EBONIZED ASH BOWL WITH METAL STUDS

H: 7in (178mm)   D: 8in (203mm)

You often see very old heavy doors made with strong studs. Some of the studs are there for the purpose of holding struts or hinges, while some do not seem to serve a purpose other than decoration. I talked about this with an architect and he said many were there just to give 'an impression of strength'.

I decided I would try to convey this in my piece by incorporating metal studs on to the rim of this rather tough-looking bowl.

A ribbed texture added to the exterior of the bowl helped to complete the rugged look.

EBONY DISH

H: 2in (51mm)   D: 13in (330mm)

I wanted to establish a link between the brown and black streaks in this lovely ebony wood. The black of the metal studs inserted into the rim achieved this for me.

Ebony works to a wonderful finish. It is a pleasure to cut and sand, as I am sure you will enjoy discovering.

SPALTED BEECH BOWL WITH LUGS
AND ROPE HANDLE

H: 7in (178mm)   D: 13in (330mm)

The bowl was cut from quite a large piece of wood allowing me spare material to carve the lugs. When it was turned it was originally 16in (406mm) wide allowing me 3in (76mm) to cut away. This left a rim at the top, which the lugs were carved from using a carving blade on a grinder.

Once the lugs were carved and sanded I had the problem of drilling holes for the rope handles. As the lugs were on a round surface I could not drill straight through. Starting with a fine drill, I gradually increased the drill sizes until I had the same drill size as the rope I wanted to use. After threading the rope through the holes, I cut it and super-glued it into the last hole.

BEECH BOWL SPRAYED BLACK WITH TEXTURED BASE AND ROPE DECORATION

H: 6½in (165mm)   D: 15in (381mm)

The rope used in this bowl was purely decorative. The previous bowl had rope handles which could be taken as functional.

After the bowl was turned, I cut a cove into the top rim in which to seat the rope. This was cut at an appropriate depth and width to accommodate the size of rope I wanted to use. I also added a ribbed texture to the base, which helped to give a good grip when handling this rather large and heavy bowl.

I was not skilful enough to splice the ends of the rope together, and so I used another natural material – leather – to cover the join. I added another piece of leather on the other side to balance the piece.

ASH BOWL WITH ROPE DECORATION

H: 4in (102mm)   D: 12in (305mm)

I turned the bowl and cut a groove of sufficient depth in the rim to take the rope I intended to use.

Again, I used spirit dye to colour the rope but I also dyed the bowl the same colour. The advantage of using dye rather than paint, is that it allows the natural grain of the ash to show through the colour.

SPALTED BEECH BOWL ON METAL STAND

H: 8in (203mm)   D: 12in (305mm)

I wanted to turn a continuous curved line to this
bowl, with no obvious base to break the line. This then
presents the problem of how to stand this kind of work.
A local museum near me exhibits many Roman
artefacts – among them large two-handled amphorae
used to carry liquids. They stand on strong metal bases.
These exhibits solved my problem for me and
I purchased several stands from a craft shop in
different sizes and shapes.

YEW HOLLOW BOTTLE ON STAND

H: 10in (254mm)   D: 3½in (89mm)

This is continuing the theme of a continuous curved line without a flat base, very much in the vein of early amphorae.

The wire spiral base was originally intended to hold a candle but I substituted a hollow bottle. I tried to complement the curve of the base with the curve of the bottle.

WALNUT, EBONY AND COCOBOLO VASE
ON METAL STAND

H: 10in (254mm)   D: 5in (127mm)

This has more of an art deco shape than the previous
bottle shape. The combination of woods at the top
continues this theme.

This piece sits in the spiral base resting on a rim that
I have cut in the walnut.

**BLACK HOLLOW BOTTLE WITH
FLAX PAPER SYMBOL**

H: 9in (229mm)   D: 3½in (89mm)

I had been influenced in turning this shape by visiting
an exhibition of Chinese art.

I tried to emulate the subtle curve on the straight-
sided ceramic vessels that I saw. I wanted to emphasize
this subtlety but the wood I used was a rather bland
piece of beech and didn't really give the effect I wanted.
So I sprayed it black using a matt black auto bumper
spray paint.

I added a handmade paper symbol which had been
produced by a craftsman from dyed flax. The character
means 'friendship'.

ASH BOWL WITH DECORATIVE RESIN RIM

H: 3in (76mm)   D: 8½in (216mm)

Having turned the bowl from well-seasoned ash using a faceplate, I cut a trench of about 9mm (⅜in) depth and 19mm (¾in) diameter. I filled this trench with a decorative resin (Inlace); the decorative material is included in the resin. You need to stir in a hardener ensuring there are no air bubbles when you pour it into the trench. It should be left proud above the trench as shrinkage will occur.

The bowl was then left on its faceplate and allowed to dry thoroughly for a couple of days. I then returned it to the lathe for finishing. I wondered whether it would cut cleanly, and what effect it would have on the edge of my tools. However I need not have concerned myself, for it cut very well and sanded beautifully.

MAHOGANY BOWL WITH DECORATIVE RESIN RIM

H: 3½in (89mm)   D: 10½in (267mm)

The resin used in this bowl was industrial resin to which I added my own decorative material: aluminium metallic powder. I had to make a judgement myself when I had added enough powder (unlike the commercially produced material which is ready-prepared for use). Once I was satisfied as to the thickness of the mixture I had to add hardener.

I wanted a slightly narrower rim on the top of the already turned bowl. I had also textured the outer edge of the bowl. Once the resin had dried it was returned to the lathe to finish. I gave the whole bowl two coats of Danish oil, including the resin.

SAPELE MAHOGANY BOWL WITH DECORATIVE RESIN RIM

H: 4in (102mm)   D: 6in (152mm)

I found it much more difficult to decorate the outer wall of a bowl than a top rim. When applying resin to the top of a bowl, providing it is on a level surface, the resin stays in the trench you have cut for it. On the outer wall it is inclined to 'slide'.

For this reason I chose to use a thicker epoxy resin to which I added a blue liquid pigment, especially designed to add to resins. I had to work much quicker with the paste resin as the drying time is very limited – but at least it stayed put once inserted into the small cove I had cut.

Squares and rectangles

Hard angles are not normally associated with 'round' woodturnings,
but they can add another dimension to our work.

It generally means 'afterwork' when you have taken the work from the
lathe, for example using a bandsaw to remove waste wood, using a table
saw to cut strips, and so on.

If you try turning sharp angles on the lathe you have to watch your hands.
It is much safer to protect the edges first and remove waste wood later.

MAHOGANY BOWL WITH ANGLED EDGES (BLANK)

H: 3in (76mm)   W: 9in (229mm)

Many turners turn angled work straight on the lathe without adding waste wood. Personally, I like to add waste wood (as illustrated above) to achieve cleaner edges, especially when sanding. It is also safer – I find sharp points spinning round at speed a bit intimidating!

The waste wood can be carefully removed after turning, using a bandsaw, finishing with a linisher or sanded by hand and applying finishing material.

This eight-sided piece was made from well-seasoned mahogany which, I think, for angled work is essential. While the movement that often occurs with wood that is not fully dry seems perfectly acceptable in rounded forms, it doesn't look so good with angles.

**MAHOGANY BOWL WITH ANGLED EDGES
(FINISHED PIECE)**

H: 3in (76mm)   W: 9in (229mm)

MAHOGANY FREE-STANDING PLAQUE ON STAND

H: 15in (381mm)   W: 16in (406mm)

Using the waste wood method, circles were cut into both sides of a block of mahogany. This would allow the work to be viewed from both sides. After removing the waste wood and cleaning up the work, the block was then cut into strips and rearranged to form a strong pattern.
(I have also included a photograph on the following page of a close-up detail of the interesting effects you can achieve using this method.)

Once I was satisfied with the pattern, I dowelled and glued each strip together.

The whole piece was mounted with round-section stainless steel onto another block of mahogany.

MAHOGANY FREE-STANDING PLAQUE ON STAND
(DETAIL)

H: 15in (381mm)   W: 16in (406mm)

SCORCHED ELM RECTANGULAR BOWL

H: 4in (102mm)   W: 4in (102mm)   L: 8in (203mm)

Unlike the preceding pieces, this bowl was turned without waste wood. The rectangular piece of elm was mounted and turned directly on the lathe.

It was then scorched with a blowtorch and brushed with a fine wire brush. Finally it was given a coat of Danish oil to produce a surface finish.

SANDBLASTED ASH SQUARE DISH

H: 3in (76mm) W: 8in (203mm) L: 8in (203mm)

I found the 'roundness' of the grain of the white ash in opposition to the 'squareness' of the dish very interesting.

I emphasized the grain structure by sandblasting the soft fibres away, leaving the hard fibres in relief.

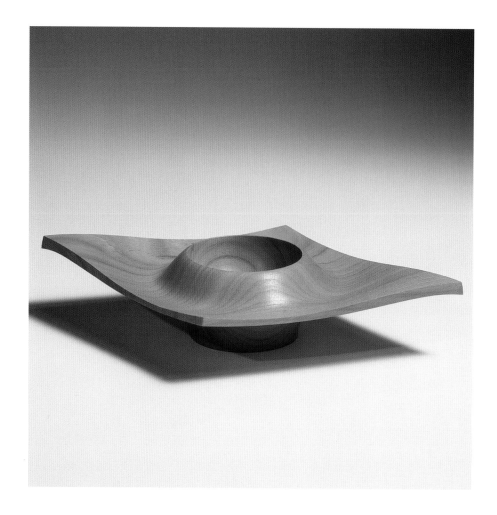

CHERRY DIAMOND-SHAPE BOWL

H: 3in (76mm)   W: 6in (152mm)   L: 6in (152mm)

Using the waste wood method, the bowl was raised out of the diamond. By turning the outer dish I was able to introduce movement to the piece. I saw this movement in an aquarium as a skate fish drifted by, and hoped I could capture this flow in a piece of woodturning.

The piece was also raised on a small foot to help to give the feeling of floating, rather than lying flat on a surface.

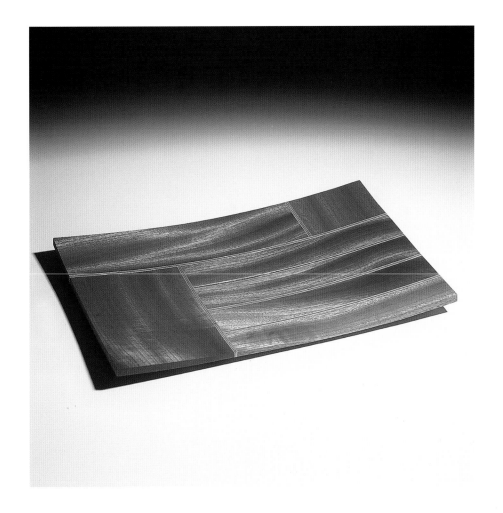

MAHOGANY AND BIRCH PLYWOOD-INSET
RECTANGULAR DISH

H: ¾in (19mm) W: 7in (178mm) L: 14in (356mm)

The different sections of square and rectangular pieces were cut from a plank of mahogany. They were separated by thin birch plywood. I glued these section-by-section before completing the rectangle.

I switched the grain patterns in opposition to one another to add movement. The turning was quite shallow – just enough to give a little depth to the dish.

PIET'S PLATTER
ASH, MAHOGANY AND PURPLEHEART

H: 1in (25mm)   W: 10in (254mm)

I have titled this piece 'Piet's Platter' to acknowledge my source: I have always admired Piet Mondrian's paintings with his use of blocks of strong contrasting colours with bold edges.

It was while turning some square-edge platters that I realised I could interpret my admiration for his work on the lathe.

It was a game of patience while laminating the work, as I had to prepare the piece in sections before finally gluing the square as a whole. Using the waste wood system around the edges while turning enabled me to achieve the clean edges I required.

MAHOGANY AND BEECH PLATTER

H: ¾in (19mm) W: 8½in (216mm) L: 12in (305mm)

I saw a flat rectangular fish platter in a restaurant
and I liked the idea of reproducing this shape in wood.
I also wanted to use contrasting woods with opposing
grain patterns.

When the piece was finished, I thought the square
corners looked rather harsh so I decided to round
them off to give a more gentle feel to the work.

ASH SQUARE RAISED-EDGE BOWL

H: 3in (76mm)   W: 6in (152mm)

This was turned directly from the square wood blank.
Care must be taken to keep the edges clean when
turning in this way.

A deep bowl and a small foot were turned. The turning
was then completed, inclining in towards the bowl which
formed the raised corners.

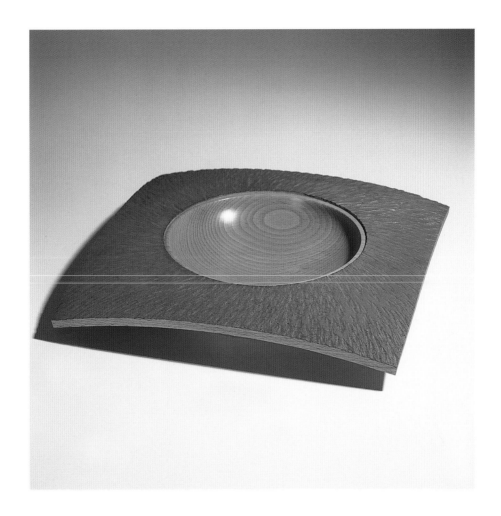

SQUARE-EDGED BEECH BOWL

H: 1½in (38mm)   W: 11in (279mm)

The waste wood method was used here. The rim of this dish inclines away from the centre to emphasize the effect of the texture flowing away from the bowl. (The texture was achieved with an Arbortech Mini Grinder, as before.)

The rim was dyed blue with a water-soluble dye. I then cut a defining rim around the bowl.

Exotics and others

I spend quite a lot of time looking for good wood to turn; I suppose I am always looking for the 'ultimate' piece. I shall be searching forever, which is part of the pleasure of woodturning.

I find burrs fascinating to work with. You never know what they are going to reveal – particularly some of the Australian burrs. Native burr oak and burr elm are two of my favourites. I enjoy the way the burrs 'pull' against the straight grain wood when drying, leaving a rippled surface which adds interest to the turned work.

Exotic timbers are among the most spectacular in colour and pattern. Although, quite rightly, there is much anxiety about the use of exotic timbers now, my suppliers assure me that the wood they offer is taken only from sustainable sources.

Natural features like 'spaltering' can produce wonderful effects and are now much sought after.

COCOBOLO HOLLOW FORM

H: 7in (178mm)   D: 7in (178mm)

This cocobolo is from the rosewood family and has a rich variety of colour streaks. It has good texture for turning. I decided to turn a hollow form which shows its beautiful features to their best advantage. I raised just a soft small lip at the top but gently curved it into the hollow.

Like all woods, tone changes will take place in time. Although the rich vibrant colours will darken, the strong grain pattern will remain.

FLAME-FIGURED OAK CLOSED FORM

H: 4in (102mm)   D: 10in (254mm)

I would not normally allow wood to dictate in what shape it should be turned. It is very easy to be beguiled by pretty wood and forget all about shape in order to show the wood.

I normally prefer to design a shape, then select wood that will work with that shape. Occasionally though, the wood itself suggests a shape and persuades me to make a shape that suits the wood, as it did in the case of this special piece of oak.

The very small lip at the top of the form directs the eye back towards the flow of the grain. Turning this piece was a very satisfying experience.

AMERICAN WALNUT VASE

H: 11in (279mm)   D: 8in (203mm)

I wanted to turn a classic vase shape and was fortunate enough to find this beautiful piece of American walnut with its striking flowing-grain patterns.

The diameter of the base and the start of the rim are the same size, which helped to give the piece its balance.

When you find a piece of wood like this the whole experience of designing and turning becomes a great pleasure!

SPALTED BEECH 'GLOBE' HOLLOW FORM

H: 6in (152mm)   D: 7in (178mm)

The useful beech, native to Europe, would hardly qualify for the word 'spectacular' but when it is spalted, it can easily be included in this category.

Some parts of the wood may be too damaged by the spaltering to turn, and this is revealed when the wood is grey in colour or spongy to the touch. If you select wood that has a fair amount of good beech left, you can produce work that people find intriguing and appealing.

BROWN BURR OAK HOLLOW FORM

H: 8in (203mm)   D: 10in (254mm)

The 'burls' or 'burrs', the rough or irregular protuberances found on a wide variety of trees, can produce some of the most interesting pieces of wood to turn. Before woodturners discovered their attractiveness they were burned, as cabinetmakers had no use for them and they tended to be a nuisance lying around in timber yards. Veneers were often cut from them but they only produced small pieces.

This piece of wood came from a very old tree in Cornwall and I felt very privileged when it was given to me.

I love the challenge of turning hollow forms and combined with this attractive wood it has become one of my favourite pieces.

TIGER STRIPE MYRTLE VASE

H: 9in (229mm)   D: 6in (152mm)

Myrtle is a very attractive wood in its usual form but this particular species is named for obvious reasons, varying greatly in colour and figure.

The vase shape gave me the opportunity of revealing its dramatic patterns.

FIGURED ACACIA HOLLOW FORM

H: 6in (152mm)   D: 9in (229mm)

This piece of wood had such potential, I had to give a lot of thought to the shape I used, so that the grain structure could be seen to its maximum effect.

I found a hollow form offered the best option in this case, and I was able to retain the 'flow' of the pattern.

QUILTED MAPLE DISH

H: 2½in (64mm)   D: 6in (152mm)

When you have paid a substantial amount of money for a piece of wood you want to get the best out of it. On studying this piece of wood, I realized that the 'quilted' effect did not seem to extend down very deep into the timber. For this reason, I decided to cut across the grain rather than cut deep into it. I turned it off-centre to allow for a small dish and a wide rim to get the best of the quilted effect.

Quilted maple is so-called because of the three-dimensional padded effect produced from the unusual grain structure. Like all the maples, it has a lovely sheen.

BELI DISCUS VASE

H: 14in (356mm)   D: 14in (356mm)

This wood is African in origin, and has very attractive subtle shaded, striped tones ranging from yellow to dark brown.

The discus shape seemed to be the right shape for this quite large wood blank. I inserted a glass tube in the body of the work so it could be functional or it could simply be accepted as a sculptural shape.

The wood finishes well with a lovely natural sheen.

MACASSAR EBONY BOWL

H: 4in (102mm)   D: 5in (127mm)

Ebony is one of the most beautiful woods to turn. It cuts so well and has a natural sheen. It is now, quite rightly, one of the protected species, and is currently very expensive, but I purchased this piece many years ago.

I chose a simple classic shape that I felt would do justice to the wood.

JARRAH BURR BOWL

H: 4½in (114mm)   D: 6½in (165mm)

Jarrah is one of the more common woods found in
Australia and is used extensively for building purposes.
The jarrah burr has become one of the favourites with
turners worldwide.

The burrs do vary in colour, but are generally very warm
in tone and mature to rich shades.

When turning burrs you need a degree of control,
as the tools are inclined to bounce off the harder parts
of the burr.

I find Danish oil is a good finish to use on this or any
burr wood as it soaks into the hollows without leaving
any residue.

EBONY BOWL

H: 1in (25mm)   D: 14in (356mm)

This is another beautiful wood to work with; it cuts and sands to a really fine finish. The dramatic changes in colour from light to dark are really striking. The drama of the piece is caused by using the sapwood as contrast.

It is quite costly to purchase but is very satisfying to turn.

Using different plywoods

I have been turning plywood for quite a few years but I am still surprised when I am asked whether it is a valid material for turning, after all, it is simply processed wood.

It has the blessing of giving freedom of size (being restricted only by the size your lathe will accommodate) and freedom of design. It can give you a wide choice of surface finishes.

Interesting variations of pattern can be achieved – depending on whether you stack and glue the wood vertically or horizontally before cutting.

It has the curse of taking the edge off tools because of the hard resin glue used in the manufacture, so it is necessary to return to the grinder to sharpen your tools more often than usual. However, this is surely a small price to pay for the luxury of working with stable material.

RAINBOW PLYWOOD BOWL
(BLANK)

H: 3in (76mm)   D: 3½in (89mm)

Rainbow plywood is manufactured in the same way
as other plywoods but each surface layer is dyed before
being glued, which gives some intriguing effects.

It has mostly been applied for small items, such
as pens, but I purchased some blocks in America
(see above) and used it as I had been using
normal plywood.

I turned this small bowl (see opposite), but I did use
a waste wood spigot as a base in order to get the
maximum depth from the blank.

**RAINBOW PLYWOOD BOWL
(FINISHED PIECE)**

H: 3in (76mm)   D: 3½in (89mm)

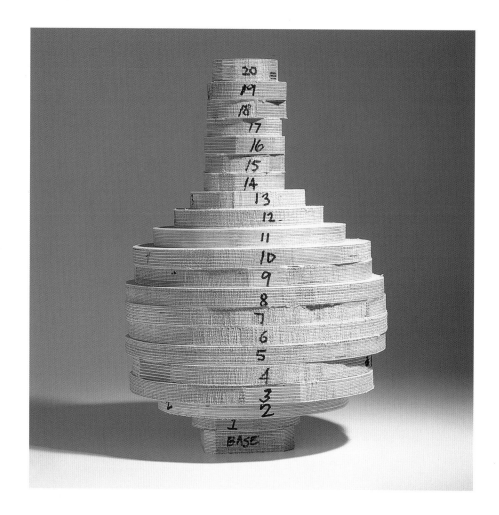

PLYWOOD FLASK
(PREPARATION)

H: 12in (305mm)   D: 12in (305mm)

The photograph above illustrates how this piece was structured. I numbered the discs of plywood to help me to keep the right sequence when gluing, and cut some of the centres out of the larger discs before gluing and hollowing.

I used PVA glue and lots of clamps during the construction. This process is fairly time consuming as the glue for each section must be allowed to dry thoroughly. I allow spare wood at the base and the top as spigots to hold the work on the lathe.

The photograph on the following page shows the final result.

PLYWOOD FLASK
(FINISHED PIECE)

H: 12in (305mm)   D: 12in (305mm)

PLYWOOD ANGLED SPHERE

H: 9in (229mm)   D: 9in (229mm)

This was produced from a block of laminated birch plywood measuring about 10 × 10in (254 × 254mm).

The spherical form allowed me to incorporate the lines created in the manufacture of plywood into the design.

After turning the sphere, hollowing a small bowl, and sanding and finishing the sphere on the lathe, it was removed and a small flat base was cut.

I carefully chose the point at which I wanted the sphere to stand, before committing myself to cutting the base. It is quite a heavy piece of work and the cut base had to be sufficient to allow it to stand without movement.

PLYWOOD HOLLOW FORM

H: 10in (254mm)   D: 14in (356mm)

I normally use birch plywood for turning, but I saw this fireproofed plywood, which was a rich brown colour, and thought it looked rather attractive. It was hollowed in two halves and then joined with a collar joint.

Whatever the added ingredient was that made it fireproof, it provided a good colour and a nice surface to finish.

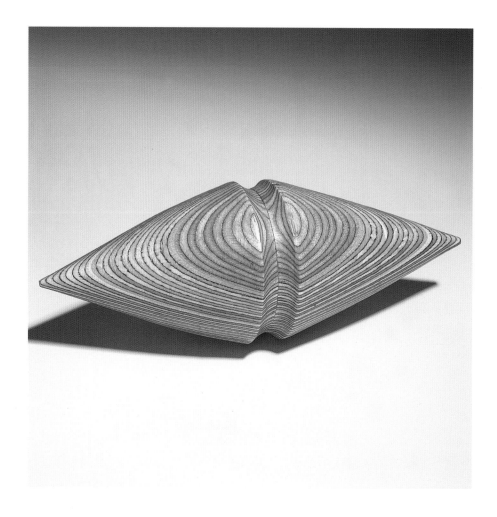

PLYWOOD 'POD' BOX

H: 4½in (114mm)   W: 10in (254mm)

I made a block of plywood strips, laminating the wood vertically which gives a good flowing pattern, as it reveals some fascia wood when cutting.

I then cut the block in two and turned and hollowed each cone. I left a rim on each cone that enabled me to insert dowels in one rim and to drill holes to meet the dowels in the other as a fixing. This enabled the cones to be pulled apart fulfilling its function as a box.

SANDBLASTED PLYWOOD FLASK

H: 10½in (267mm)   D: 5½in (140mm)

This was turned in two pieces, as previously described.

Rather than giving it a smooth finish, I decided to sandblast the exterior to produce a strong texture to the surface. The sandblasting also had the effect of making it one tone, which somehow added to the interest of the piece.

GROUP OF 3 PLYWOOD BOXES

A DRUM   H: 7in (178mm)   D: 3½in (89mm)
B TRIANGLE   H: 11in (279mm)   W: 6in (152mm)
C SPHERE   H: 4½in (114mm)   D: 4½in (114mm)

Groups of shapes have been produced in all kinds of material: stone, glass, plastic, metal. It seems to be a standard exercise that most craftspeople produce during their lives.

These boxes are all hollow and constructed from laminated birch plywood blocks.

I tried to get a relationship between the shapes and the sizes, and drew them out several times before I was satisfied with the measurements.

LARGE PLYWOOD HOLLOW FORM

H: 15in (381mm)   D: 17in (432mm)

This was hollowed and turned in two halves from structured plywood with a collar joint to connect the hollowed pieces. The top piece is inset and glued into a collar cut into the bottom piece. This was quite a large piece of work to finish on the lathe, although surprisingly light to handle.

Once it had been joined (while it was still on its spigot) I sanded and finished the outside and gave the exterior a ribbed surface using a ¼in high-speed steel tool bit mounted in a ½in steel rod in a wooden handle, ground to a 'fingernail' shape. It was then removed from its spigot to take off the lathe. The exterior was coated with matt acrylic paint which is a good surface to keep clean.

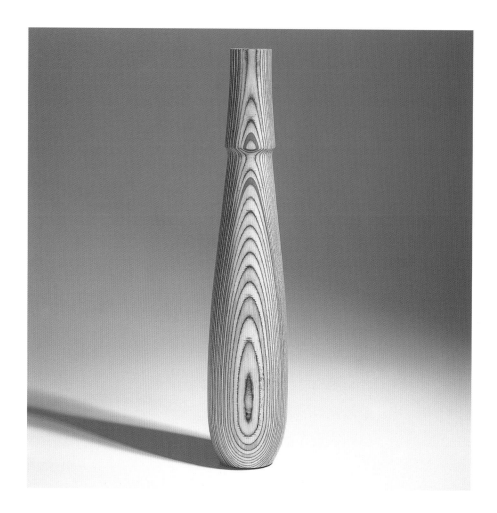

PLYWOOD AND VENEER TALL VASE

H: 17in (432mm)   D: 3in (76mm)

While laminating small lengths of birch plywood together, I incorporated some strips of coloured veneer the same width as the plywood. This time I used the length of the plywood rather than the width to achieve the effect I desired.

The colour strip graduates from narrow at the base to wide at the top, following the interesting blocks of shape that the plywood itself produces.

PLYWOOD SCULPTURAL FORM

H: 12in (305mm)   W: 9in (229mm)

Sculptors and potters often produce 'pierced work', which allows light to fall on different planes. I enjoyed the challenge of photographing this kind of work.

I decided to try a piece of turning based on the concept of 'the hole'. Turning the sphere was quite straightforward, but it then had to be remounted on the lathe from two directions to produce the different planes. It was quite heavy and had to be mounted on a base using a stainless steel rod.

Not only did I enjoy turning the piece, but I also took great pleasure in lighting the piece before photographing it.

Laminated work

A cabinetmaker friend often supplies me with offcuts of some very nice timber. Unless it is rescued it can finish up on the fire!

It is generally in thin plank form with one or two slightly thicker pieces – not deep enough to turn 'in the round'. I have found that, with patience, and enough adhesive and clamps, I can form sections that produce some interesting work.

As it comes from a cabinetmaker, it is well-seasoned timber to start with. It must be carefully planed before gluing and I work out what I want to do before I commit myself to the gluing stage.

PREPARED BLANK

The picture above shows a block of prepared strips of wood. I can either use this as it stands and turn a simple platter or cut this block into strips and incorporate them into other designs.

I can then cut this either diagonally or straight to give a variation of pattern, as shown in some of the photographs that follow.

SQUARE PLATTER
VARIETY OF WOODS

H: 1in (25mm)   L: 10in (254mm)   W: 8in (203mm)

Using a section of the prepared blank as previously
illustrated, I turned a simple shallow platter.

The edges were rounded to give a softer appearance
to the piece.

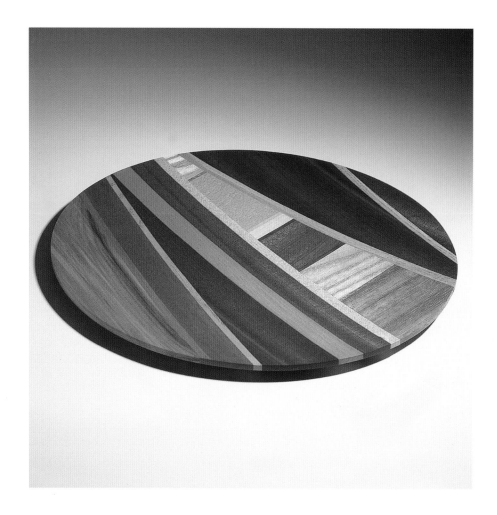

ROUND PLATTER
VARIETY OF WOODS

H: 1in (25mm)   D: 13in (330mm)

Strong diagonals give powerful movement to this platter. The sections were glued together before being bandsawn into a circle for turning in the normal way. I used a glued waste wood spigot on the base to give as much depth as possible to the piece.

You need to allow a fair amount of time to produce this kind of work. The time taken for preparation, planing and gluing in sequence, is far longer than the actual turning time!

MAHOGANY, BIRCH PLYWOOD AND WENGE
TALL RIMMED VASE

H: 14in (356mm)   D: 3½in (89mm)

This was a hollowed, structured piece. Each disc was laminated with the plywood and hollowed out. The discs were glued ½in (13mm) off-centre to the previous disc giving a 'brick wall' appearance.

The base was left as plain mahogany and the final rim disc was a piece of wenge which was left wider than the body of the work.

TULIPTREE AND MAHOGANY DEEP BOWL

H: 7in (178mm)   D: 10½in (267mm)

These were offcut blocks of tuliptree which had been prepared to turn newel posts. I defined the blocks using thick veneers of mahogany and glued them all together in a square to allow me to turn this quite deep bowl.

MAHOGANY AND BIRCH PLYWOOD BOWL

H: 4in (102mm)   D: 11in (279mm)

These again were offcuts of a well-seasoned mahogany, and I defined the blocks using a very thin birch plywood.

I have glued the blocks to give different grain directions. It is interesting to see the straight lines of the birch plywood giving way to curves as you turn the interior.

MULTI-WOOD BOWL

H: 3½in (89mm)   D: 7in (178mm)

Many offcuts were glued together and, when turned,
produced weird and wonderful shapes and patterns.
Strong ovals and contrasts appeared as turning took
place and these cut across straight lines which
I found intriguing.

WALNUT BOWL

H: 4in (102mm) D: 4in (102mm)

I found a small walnut plank about ½in (13mm) thick where the heartwood and the sapwood were very clearly defined. I kept looking at it for a long time wondering how I could use it to its best advantage. It was only 4in (102mm) across so it was not wide enough to turn a platter and was not deep enough to turn a box or a bowl.

I eventually cut it into 4in (102mm) blocks and glued them together, alternately showing the heartwood first to the right and then to the left, and the sapwood first to the left and then to the right. It made quite an attractive little bowl from a small plank.

WENGE AND MAHOGANY TALL HOLLOW VASE

H: 16in (406mm)   D: 3in (76mm)

I keep all sorts of small pieces of wood which I can't bear to throw away! Groups of these two woods were laying side-by-side on my bench and I thought what a good contrast they made with one another. The mahogany has a lovely sheen to it which goes well with the dramatic dark colour of the wenge.

Individually I could do very little with such small pieces but gluing them together in a structured shape gave me the opportunity to produce this hollow form.

BEECH AND MAHOGANY STRUCTURED OVOID

H: 16½in (419mm)   D: 5½in (140mm)

I first turned 6in (152mm) discs from the beech and mahogany. I then glued sections together and, when the glue dried, hollowed each section leaving the base section solid. The sections were then glued together and shaped on the lathe.

PURPLEHEART AND MAHOGANY TALL WEED POT

H: 19½in (495mm)   D: 4in (102mm)

These woods were in plank form – the purpleheart
about 2in (51mm) thick and the mahogany about
1in (25mm) thick. I layered the mahogany between the
purpleheart and glued them together for turning.

After completion I simply drilled a hole down through
the work.

The purple colour will tone down but will still retain
a strong, warm colour.

TULIPWOOD, OAK AND MAHOGANY BOTTLE

H: 18½in (470mm)   D: 5½in (140mm)

I laminated planks of different widths of wood together to produce this striped effect. Tulipwood also has its own stripes of different colours ranging from light to dark, and so I placed this in the centre.

As you turn, of course, the 'straightness' of the planked wood disappears, to produce ovals and rounds which are very effective in opposition to the uprights.

Off-centre turning

If you harvest your own timber, or are given pieces of wood from a garden, you may find yourself with some oddly shaped pieces of timber. You can use this eccentricity of form if you are prepared to accept the problem of uneven weight distribution when turning.

Another way of achieving eccentricity is by using an eccentric chuck or by re-positioning a faceplate. The headstock on the lathe can only revolve in a true circular motion but if you work with a faceplate, or an eccentric chuck, you can achieve some interesting variations from 'the round'. I find that the eccentric chucks now commercially available, are ideal for small items of work, but for larger and heavier pieces, I need the strength of a faceplate with long screws into the wood to effect a good hold.

On larger pieces, the main cylinder of the work is turned in the usual way, using a faceplate with a true centre fixing. Once the main body has been completed, the faceplate is shifted away from the true centre to a point of your choosing depending on the amount of eccentricity you wish to show.

This produces a cylinder which, when revolving, is heavier on one side than the other. This can cause vibration, and I have my lathe braced both to a wall and to the floor to compensate for this.

SPALTED HORNBEAM OFF-CENTRE BUD VASE

H: 11in (279mm)   D: 5in (127mm)

This was a fairly hefty blank to start with and so I used a 6in (150mm) faceplate. I have drilled more holes than are usually provided in a commercially produced faceplate, so that I could use more screws to obtain a really strong fix to the lathe.

After turning the main body, I removed the work from the lathe and re-positioned the faceplate to a point about ¾in (19mm) away from the true centre. This was then returned to the lathe to allow me to turn the small spout off-centre at the top. I drilled a long hole down through the spout which could accommodate dried flowers to give the piece a function if required.

PITCH PINE OFF-CENTRE BOTTLE

H: 10in (254mm)   D: 3½in (89mm)

The lines that appear in pitch pine normally, have become accentuated as a result of becoming elongated. The gentle sloping movement leads the eye up to the tall spout where a small repeat pattern appears at the top. Eccentric turning has transformed a fairly ordinary piece of wood into something interesting.

Danish oil has been used to finish the piece and this helps to emphasize the darker lines of the grain structure.

ASH OFF-CENTRE DISH

H: 2½in (64mm)   D: 9in (229mm)

The blank of wood was first turned into a normal round
bowl shape using a faceplate. The faceplate was then
moved away about ¾in (19mm) from its central position.
A small raised-lip bowl was turned from this point.

The whole effect is to show the lovely flowing movement
of ash grain to its full potential.

WALNUT SPOUT BOWL

H: 4in (102mm)   D: 7in (178mm)

The flowing movement of the walnut grain and the eccentric positioning of the spout have combined to give a rather surreal effect to this piece.

A hole is drilled down the spout after the work is finished so that it could be used to display foliage or dried flowers.

MAHOGANY OFF-CENTRE BOTTLE

H: 12in (305mm)   D: 5in (127mm)

The base has been turned while the work is held on with a faceplate in a central position. The bottom part of the base has been narrowed and kept smooth, and the top part of the base has been textured to remind us of the bark of a tree.

Re-positioning the faceplate to an off-centre position, a gentle slope has been introduced, leading to the tall spout where texture has been repeated on the top.

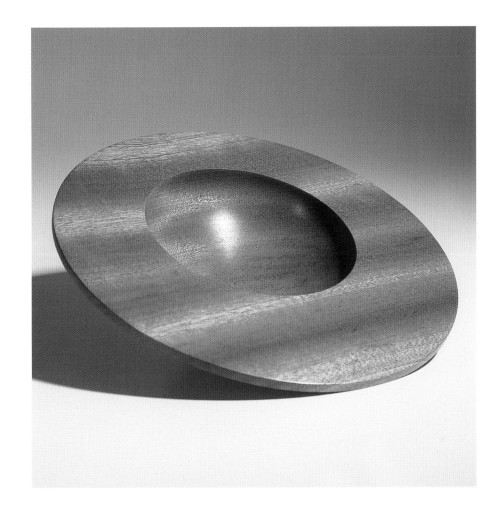

MAHOGANY DISH

H: 4in (102mm)   D: 11in (279mm)

A depth of at least 4in (102mm) of wood was necessary to achieve the effect I desired. The mahogany blank was turned to a cylinder, centrally positioned on a faceplate, then re-positioned off-centre and the small bowl hollowed.

The work was then held by large wood jaws (which were mounted onto a chuck) to enable the base to be completed. This base was then turned to a cone shape, allowing the bowl to rest at an angle on the wider part of the rim.

JARRAH OFF-CENTRE BOWL

H: 2½in (64mm)   D: 7in (178mm)

This was a rich, dark, rather brittle piece of jarrah which somehow suggested that it did not need a 'pretty' treatment but should be left fairly rugged and tough looking.

It was turned on a faceplate first and the faceplate was re-positioned to an off-centre point that allowed me to leave quite a wide rim.

I spend quite a lot of my time looking at my wood blanks before I start to turn, to get the feel of how they should be treated. Some require to be turned delicately and others, such as this piece, can accept a stronger approach.

ASH OFF-CENTRE BOWL

H: 3in (76mm)   D: 9½in (241mm)

Ash grain is very attractive and I am always seeking ways to reveal it at its best. By turning a 'doughnut' shape and then off-centring the small bowl, the grain appears to be constantly flowing in several ways giving many points of interest.

When the shape is finished, the work is reversed on the lathe to complete a perfectly plain base with no ugly chuck or spigot marks.

AFRORMOSIA OFF-CENTRE BOTTLE

H: 11in (279mm)   D: 5in (127mm)

The long grain of this blank influenced me when deciding on the form it should take. I wanted to keep one of the strong 'lines' running right up from the base to the top and it was this that made up my mind where the spout should be placed. Having made this decision I kept the rest of the shape very simple.

Although I drilled a long hole down into the piece so that it could be used in some way, people seem to be quite happy to accept the work simply as sculptural form.

NATURAL EDGE ASH BOWL

H: 4in (102mm)   W: 12in (305mm)

Nature is very rarely perfectly symmetrical and sometimes it can be very eccentric! The log was quite thin at one end and thick at the other. The faceplate had to be placed on the thicker end which, of course, made it off-balance on the lathe but because my lathe is braced, it coped with this unevenly weighted piece.

I turned a small bowl leaving the bark on the rim and outside edge. Once the piece had been finished and sanded, the bark was brushed and the whole work was given several coats of Danish oil.

MAHOGANY AND BIRCH PLYWOOD SPOUT VASE

H: 12in (305mm)   D: 4in (102mm)

This was a structured piece made up from discs of
mahogany with very thin birch plywood between the
discs. As it was built up, I was able to hollow each disc.
The spout was not laminated.

The vase itself was turned centrally but when
I had finally glued the top it was re-positioned on the
faceplate to off-centre the spout. I did not slope the
body of the vase but the spout was gently curved
leading up to the rim.

MULBERRY RIMMED BOWL

H: 5½in (140mm)   W: 9in (229mm)

This rather knobbly, broken piece of mulberry challenged me to do something with it! It was quite eccentric but I wanted to use that element. I turned away part of the base but left a rim of natural bark. I then turned a section above the rim, even though it was broken into – it was not an easy piece to turn!

On completion, I brushed it very vigorously and then gave it four or five coats of Danish oil to give a nice warm tone.

Just shape and form

Simplicity has great appeal but it is often the hardest thing to achieve. Simple shapes and designs can be truly beautiful, relying totally on perfect curves, good lines and the right proportions.

If these things are not quite right, the work is under par. We all try hard to get there but often just miss out – just keep on trying and never give in!

HOLLY VASE

H: 8½in (216mm)   D: 5½in (140mm)

Holly is an even-textured wood and can be almost white. It does, unfortunately, have a tendency to split, but I was lucky with this piece. This was rough-turned and left for a year to dry before re-turning.

I tried to achieve an ovoid simplicity, reflecting the eggshell-like colour of the wood. I left it as a matt finish because of this.

The sides are not absolutely straight but curve slightly inward towards the top.

BURR OAK BOWL

H: 3in (76mm)   D: 13in (330mm)

I turned a simple bowl shape from this nice piece
of burr, and made a rim with a slight decline to give
movement at the top of the piece.

It was a warm rich colour and responded well to
several coats of Danish oil.

CHERRY BOWL

H: 4½in (114mm)   D: 9in (229mm)

This piece of native cherry has a very nice figure to it. Cherry, when drying from 'wet', has a tendency to split at any stage in the drying process. My normal method of turning any wood, is to rough-turn each piece to an inch (25mm) thick and leave it in this state for about a year or so.

With cherry, I have to examine it many times during this drying time to make sure that it has not split.

I left a small foot on the bowl to 'lift' it so that the shape of the bowl could be seen at its best.

PLUM HOLLOW FORM

H: 9in (229mm)   D: 7in (178mm)

The grain structure of this wood suggested to me long-grain turning in order to capture the strong lines and differing tones.

It was turned in one, using a hollowing hook tool. The small rim at the top gave a completion to this very simple shape.

BURR ELM BOWL

H: 4in (102mm)   D: 7in (178mm)

A small bowl with a wide rim seemed to show this wood at its best. The wood had lots of life and movement within its structure, while the warm tone was bought to life when it was finished with three coats of Danish oil, allowing 24 hours' drying between each coat.

PAIR OF GOBLETS
YEW AND ROSEWOOD

H: 11in (279mm)   D: 3in (76mm)

The simple elegance of the goblet shape is
very appealing – it is a shape that many turners
enjoy turning.

I do very little spindle turning but I found making
these pieces to be very pleasurable.

IROKO 'DOUGHNUT' BOWL

H: 4in (102mm)   D: 13in (330mm)

The rolling curves of a doughnut were the inspiration for this piece of work; you are unable to distinguish where the curve begins and ends. It is a lovely rounded, sensual shape – very tactile.

COCOBOLO BOWL

H: 3½in (89mm)   D: 9½in (241mm)

Cocobolo is a beautiful wood, and so in order to respect that I kept the shape as simple and as elegant as possible. An enclosed form allows you to bring the sides into the centre keeping the flow to the grain structure. A straight-sided bowl sometimes interrupts the flow, whereas a hollow form or enclosed form allows the contours to flow freely.

WHITE RIBBED OPEN BOWL – PLYWOOD

H: 9in (229m)   D: 15in (381mm)

This large bowl was turned from a block of laminated birch plywood measuring 10 × 16in (254 × 406mm).

After turning, I left an area of about 1in (25mm) on the outside of the bowl at the top and base which I kept smooth. The area between these two was ribbed using a fine gouge, and the inside was left smooth.

The whole bowl was painted with acrylic white paint which seemed to be complementary to the simplicity of the shape.

FIGURED MAPLE VASE

H: 9in (229mm)   D: 7½in (191mm)

I used a hollowing tool to produce this form, as this enabled me to reach into the limited space available to cut the curved part of the shoulder of the vessel.

Maple is one of the lightest toned woods with a lovely natural sheen to it. It only needs the palest oil or polish to bring out this effect.

It is a good-natured wood to work with and doesn't cause too many problems!

JARRAH WIDE-RIMMED BOWL

H: 3in (76mm)   D: 8in (203mm)

I was keen not to detract from the strong colour of this wood and the good proportions of the blank which I had purchased, so I went for a simple, chunky shape with a strong rim.

The power of this wood is in both the colour and its granular structure. These features lend themselves well to the simplicity of a wide-rimmed bowl. The wide top allows the eye to follow the continuous movement of the grain throughout the bowl.

SPALTED ELM DEEP BOWL

H: 8in (203mm)   D: 7in (178mm)

The deep bowl shape is very satisfying to turn,
being a simple and very natural form.

The rim was raised slightly to add some interest and
movement and to give a crisp edge to the bowl itself.

Bibliography

Child, Peter, *The Craftsman Woodturner* (Revised Edition, GMC Publications, Lewes, 1997)

Irons, Phil, *Woodturning: Two Books in One* (Sterling/Silver, New York, 1999; Apple, London, 2000)

Le Coff, Albert, *Lathe Turned Objects* (Wood Turning Center, Philadelphia, 1985)

Nish, Dale, *Artistic Woodturning* (Stobart & Son, London, 1981)

Nish, Dale, *Creative Woodturning* (Brigham Young University Press, 1975; Stobart & Son, London, 1976)

Pain, Frank, *The Practical Woodturner* (Evans Bros., London, 1957; Revised Edition, HarperCollins, London, 1993)

Pye, David, *Woodcarver and Turner* (Bell & Hyman, London, 1957)

Raffan, Richard, *Turned Bowl Design* (Taunton Press, Connecticut, 1987; Unwin Hyman, London, 1988)

Rowley, Keith, *Woodturning: A Foundation Course* (New Edition, GMC Publications, Lewes, 1999)

Sainsbury, John, *John Sainsbury's Guide to Woodturning Tools and Equipment* (David & Charles, London, 1989)

About the Author

For most of his working life, John Hunnex was a professional photographer, in particular photographing artists' work for publication. In addition to exhibiting his own photographic work at various venues, he was invited to lecture at Goldsmiths College School of Art in London, where he worked for 17 years, nurturing his creative talents.

He has been turning wood as a hobby for over 40 years alongside his profession as a photographer and, since moving to the country with his wife Rose upon retirement, has devoted most of his time to woodturning. He enjoys producing a wide variety of pieces in both native and exotic woods – trying always for the 'unusual'.

He demonstrated for a number of years at many venues and has exhibited his work widely throughout England. His work has also been featured in various magazines, including *Woodturning*.

TITLES AVAILABLE FROM
GMC Publications
BOOKS

WOODCARVING

Beginning Woodcarving   *GMC Publications*
Carving Architectural Detail in Wood: The Classical Tradition
    Frederick Wilbur
Carving Birds & Beasts   *GMC Publications*
Carving the Human Figure: Studies in Wood and Stone
    Dick Onians
Carving Nature: Wildlife Studies in Wood   *Frank Fox-Wilson*
Carving on Turning   *Chris Pye*
Celtic Carved Lovespoons: 30 Patterns
    Sharon Littley & Clive Griffin
Decorative Woodcarving (New Edition)   *Jeremy Williams*
Elements of Woodcarving   *Chris Pye*
Essential Woodcarving Techniques   *Dick Onians*
Figure Carving in Wood: Human and Animal Forms
    Sara Wilkinson
Lettercarving in Wood: A Practical Course   *Chris Pye*
Relief Carving in Wood: A Practical Introduction   *Chris Pye*
Woodcarving for Beginners   *GMC Publications*
Woodcarving Made Easy   *Cynthia Rogers*
Woodcarving Tools, Materials & Equipment
(New Edition in 2 vols.)   *Chris Pye*

WOODTURNING

Bowl Turning Techniques Masterclass   *Tony Boase*
Chris Child's Projects for Woodturners   *Chris Child*
Contemporary Turned Wood: New Perspectives
in a Rich Tradition   *Ray Leier, Jan Peters & Kevin Wallace*
Decorating Turned Wood: The Maker's Eye
    Liz & Michael O'Donnell
Green Woodwork   *Mike Abbott*
Intermediate Woodturning Projects   *GMC Publications*
Keith Rowley's Woodturning Projects   *Keith Rowley*
Making Screw Threads in Wood   *Fred Holder*
Segmented Turning: A Complete Guide   *Ron Hampton*
Turned Boxes: 50 Designs   *Chris Stott*
Turning Green Wood   *Michael O'Donnell*
Turning Pens and Pencils   *Kip Christensen & Rex Burningham*
Woodturning: Forms and Materials   *John Hunnex*
Woodturning: A Foundation Course (New Edition)   *Keith Rowley*
Woodturning: A Fresh Approach   *Robert Chapman*
Woodturning: An Individual Approach   *Dave Regester*
Woodturning: A Source Book of Shapes   *John Hunnex*
Woodturning Masterclass   *Tony Boase*
Woodturning Techniques   *GMC Publications*

WOODWORKING

Beginning Picture Marquetry   *Lawrence Threadgold*
Celtic Carved Lovespoons: 30 Patterns
    Sharon Littley & Clive Griffin
Celtic Woodcraft   *Glenda Bennett*
Complete Woodfinishing (Revised Edition)   *Ian Hosker*
David Charlesworth's Furniture-Making Techniques
    David Charlesworth
David Charlesworth's Furniture-Making
Techniques – Volume 2   *David Charlesworth*

Furniture-Making Projects for the Wood Craftsman
    GMC Publications
Furniture-Making Techniques for the Wood Craftsman
    GMC Publications
Furniture Projects with the Router   *Kevin Ley*
Furniture Restoration (Practical Crafts)   *Kevin Jan Bonner*
Furniture Restoration: A Professional at Work   *John Lloyd*
Furniture Restoration and Repair for Beginners *Kevin Jan Bonner*
Furniture Restoration Workshop   *Kevin Jan Bonner*
Green Woodwork   *Mike Abbott*
Intarsia: 30 Patterns for the Scrollsaw   *John Everett*
Kevin Ley's Furniture Projects   *Kevin Ley*
Making Chairs and Tables – Volume 2   *GMC Publications*
Making Classic English Furniture   *Paul Richardson*
Making Heirloom Boxes   *Peter Lloyd*
Making Screw Threads in Wood   *Fred Holder*
Making Woodwork Aids and Devices   *Robert Wearing*
Mastering the Router   *Ron Fox*
Pine Furniture Projects for the Home   *Dave Mackenzie*
Router Magic: Jigs, Fixtures and Tricks to
Unleash your Router's Full Potential   *Bill Hylton*
Router Projects for the Home   *GMC Publications*
Router Tips & Techniques   *Robert Wearing*
Routing: A Workshop Handbook   *Anthony Bailey*
Routing for Beginners   *Anthony Bailey*
Sharpening: The Complete Guide   *Jim Kingshott*
Space-Saving Furniture Projects   *Dave Mackenzie*
Stickmaking: A Complete Course   *Andrew Jones & Clive George*
Stickmaking Handbook   *Andrew Jones & Clive George*
Storage Projects for the Router   *GMC Publications*
Veneering: A Complete Course   *Ian Hosker*
Veneering Handbook   *Ian Hosker*
Woodworking Techniques and Projects   *Anthony Bailey*
Woodworking with the Router: Professional
Router Techniques any Woodworker can Use
    Bill Hylton & Fred Matlack

UPHOLSTERY

Upholstery: A Complete Course (Revised Edition)   *David James*
Upholstery Restoration   *David James*
Upholstery Techniques & Projects   *David James*
Upholstery Tips and Hints   *David James*

TOYMAKING

Scrollsaw Toy Projects   *Ivor Carlyle*
Scrollsaw Toys for All Ages   *Ivor Carlyle*

DOLLS' HOUSES AND MINIATURES

1/12 Scale Character Figures for the Dolls' House
    James Carrington
Americana in 1/12 Scale: 50 Authentic Projects
    Joanne Ogreenc & Mary Lou Santovec
The Authentic Georgian Dolls' House   *Brian Long*
A Beginners' Guide to the Dolls' House Hobby   *Jean Nisbett*

CRAFTS

GARDENING

PHOTOGRAPHY

ART TECHNIQUES

VIDEOS

MAGAZINES

WOODTURNING ◆ WOODCARVING ◆ FURNITURE & CABINETMAKING
THE ROUTER ◆ NEW WOODWORKING ◆ THE DOLLS' HOUSE MAGAZINE
OUTDOOR PHOTOGRAPHY ◆ BLACK & WHITE PHOTOGRAPHY
TRAVEL PHOTOGRAPHY ◆ MACHINE KNITTING NEWS
GUILD OF MASTER CRAFTSMEN NEWS

The above represents a full list of all titles currently published or scheduled to be published.
All are available direct from the Publishers or through bookshops, newsagents and specialist retailers.
To place an order, or to obtain a complete catalogue, contact:

GMC Publications,
Castle Place, 166 High Street, Lewes, East Sussex BN7 1XU United Kingdom
Tel: 01273 488005 Fax: 01273 402866
E-mail: pubs@thegmcgroup.com

Orders by credit card are accepted